FROM THE AUTHOR:

For as long as I can remember, I attended church with my family and I was baptized at the age of 8 years old. Yet, I lost my way like the prodigal son. In my wilderness experience I found myself as a high school drop-out, chasing fool's gold and self-medicating to escape reality. I was an adolescent with limited education and skills, living domestically, working hard labor and dead end jobs for a living. Now, as an adult I know that a lack of education and incarceration goes hand-in-hand; the less education the less access to economic success is desired.

In a moment of reflection, I realized I squandered the wealth of instruction and the potential of going to college on a football and track scholarship. I allowed an abnormal culture become my reality, as this negative lifestyle took root, I felt hopeless as my life spiraled out of control.

Then one night I gave up and made the horrible decision, which lead to my incarceration. In prison with a death sentence, I was faced with many thoughts and the reality of my actions and realized it was no one's fault I sat in prison but my own accounts. From the moment most people get caught for a crime they are sorry they got caught, and start thinking of themselves as a victim. I learned that this thinking only breeds negative energy and stagnated growth in moving forward towards change. I began to see the point of view of other people and how my actions affected them. I was no longer sorry I got caught.

I was sorry for those whose rights and liberties I violated. And I realized why it is said in the Bible, to love your neighbors and do unto others as you would like to be done unto you, because we are all connected in one way or another. Then I made the decision to follow and serve God. On the road to redemption and transformation I had a 'road to Damascus' experience; where I took responsibility for my life and actions, past, present and future. I discovered who I was in the body of Jesus Christ and

(continued)

began doing my part in the ministry to make a difference within the prison walls and in the communities. I found the need to write this handbook, "Things Ministers Should Think About When Ministering Behind Prison Walls."

Humbly Written,

/s/ Raymond L. Carr, Jr.

Raymond Leon Carr, Jr.

TOPICS OF DISCUSSION

SAVING SOULS

DELIVERANCE AND INNER HEALING

PREPARING TO LIVE SAVED IN A FREE SOCIETY, WHILE STILL INCARCERATED

BREAKING THE CYCLE OF INCARCERATION

MENTORING INCARCERATED SAINTS

COUNTY JAIL MINISTRY vs. PRISON MINISTRY

DATING AND COURTING IN THE CHURCH

MEN AND WOMEN IN PRISON MINISTRY

"Things Ministers Should Think About When Ministering Behind Prison Walls."

Ministering behind prison walls is a very special and unique calling in ministry; it is my intent, to share the following information in hopes that it will enlighten ministers and reduce the recidivism rate through awareness. I will endeavor to paint for you a true picture of what we, (referring to those of us who are incarcerated) need and what really goes on within us (in our thought process) inside of these prison walls. For example, it should be obvious that everyone in prison wants to get out, yet many are not prepared mentally, emotionally and spiritually to deal with the realities of the real world. This is part of the reason why the recidivism rate is so high.

In this handbook, I will address many facts and truths that will be of great benefit to anyone called to do prison ministry. Although everything I address herein may not be directly applicable to you and/or your ministry, I believe you will be enlightened and inspired by it.

There may be a lot of people who are in prison ministry who have numerous questions regarding what actually go on behind prison walls. However, often, depending on the source, the information and stories they receive are either merely half-truths, or lopsided and bias.

Through experience, I have learned that those in prison are often arbitrarily categorized as hopeless, untrustworthy, and looked upon as a collective rather than as individuals. Those of us in prison are commonly all put into the same boat and looked upon through a tainted window, with a stereotypical tint that gives a polluted perception of each person's potential as an individual. The positive aspects involving prisoners as 'Returning Citizens' are rarely made known to the general public through the news outlets or over the airwaves. Most of the time you never hear about the 'Returning Citizens' who are true success stories, who upon release have gone on to live a wholesome productive life. The public is often told about those that return to prison, but seldom, if ever, told about those who have become pastors, assistant pastors, church choir directors, Bible school teachers, or started successful businesses. The media and the 'system' paint a picture of prison that is inaccurate in many ways. I'm sure that before you, as a volunteer, were allowed into a prison, you were warned by prison staff, in a negative light, about the people you would be ministering to. However, through observation you have also likely learned that there is great diversity within the prison population and that the stereotypes are not necessarily all true.

A day in the life of most incarcerated people is a vicious cycle of repetition, wherein each day is pretty much a carbon copy of the previous day and wherein birthdays and holidays are just another day on the calendar. Even though the days are pretty much the same, each day holds its own potential and you can make of it what you will.

There are many types of incarcerated people in this environment. Some have wrong motives and hidden agendas. Some read more into a given situation then there actually is. Some are angry, frustrated, depressed, or bitter, and are not trying to change. However, there are also those of us who have been quickened together with Christ through a changed heart (Eph. 2:1-6), and the renewing of the mind (Eph. 4:22-24; Rom. 12:1, 2). Those of us who see that what we are now going through is not only a test; but a challenge of love, faithfulness, and strengthening. A time of self-examination, reflection, and devotion to learning to walk godly in righteousness toward, and in the life foreordained for us by God our Father. It is for this purpose then that I offer the following:

SAVING SOULS

"...*he that winneth souls is wise*" (Proverbs 11:30).

The reason God calls people into prison ministry is to save lost souls by preaching the Gospel ("The Good News") to every creature (Mk. 16:15). The Gospel of Jesus Christ is the power of God unto Salvation to **everyone** that believes (Rom. 1:16). To preach the kingdom of God (Mk. 1:14, 15), and obedience (Mt. 28:19, 20), even as Christ learned obedience by the things He suffered (Heb. 5:8), and the casting down of imaginations and every high thing that exalts itself against the knowledge of God, bringing into captivity every thought to the obedience of Christ (2 Cor. 10:5), the only name under heaven by which man can be saved (Acts 4:17).

No matter whether a person is free or bond (incarcerated) it is only through faith in Jesus Christ that we become children of God and heirs of the promise (Gal. 3:26-28). It is the preaching of the word of faith that becomes planted within the heart that brings about belief and confession unto salvation unto all that call upon the name of the Lord (Rom. 10:8-13). However, as the Word of God tells us, "How then shall they call upon him whom they have not believed? And how shall they believe in him of whom they have not heard? And how shall they hear without a preacher? And how shall they preach, except they be sent? As it is written, How beautiful are the feet of them that preach the gospel of peace, and bring good tidings of good things; but they have not all obeyed the gospel. For Isaiah said, Lord, who hath believed our report? So then faith cometh by hearing; and hearing by the Word of God." (Rom. 10:14-17)

In a perfect world, everyone who is ministered to would receive salvation and we would all live happily ever after. However because some, instead of placing the emphasis on the great importance of a personal, intimate, loving relationship with the Lord (Mt. 10:37, 38), have placed the emphasis on religious spiritual experiences, i.e. being slain in the spirit, seeing a vision or angel, the gifts of the Spirit, etc., therefore, many never truly enjoy the intimacy of a true personal relationship with the Lord. Although these experiences are of great importance, absent a true, personal, intimate, loving relationship with the Lord most people find it extremely difficult to simply be obedient in all things. For this reason, many have taken a nonchalant attitude towards the things of God and there is no urgency for living righteously before God. These attitudes are prevalent both outside and inside of prison. For many, attending church services are nothing more than 'something to do as a means to alleviate boredom.' For others, church services are nothing more than a tradition they have to tolerate once a week. Others, who are disobedient to God all week-long, attend church services hoping to receive a blessing just for showing up. There are countless reasons people attend church services, the vast majority of which have nothing at all to do with a righteous standing before God. Church should never be a mere hobby, or a source of entertainment, nor should it ever become simply a waiting room for Christians waiting to go to heaven. We must always keep in mind that God will not be mocked and we will reap what we sow (Gal. 6:7-9).

Both believers and unbelievers alike want to get out of prison. Vast amounts of time are spent preaching about how God will help us, bless us, and meet our every need. People flock to churches everywhere (inside and outside of prison) wanting to hear about what God will do for them. Week after week they are told to have faith in God and He will meet your need. Although it is true that God meets our every need, there are conditions to His doing so, that are not being preached. What is not being preached is the necessity of having a true, intimate, personal, loving, relationship with Christ, what God's law, commandments, statutes, and ordinances are and how to walk in them in righteousness and obedience. For this reason, people everywhere, instead of being obedient children of God who are truly blessed, merely attempt to use God for what He can do. By not walking in righteousness and obedience they are therefore walking in sin, which is death (Rom. 6:23). Therefore, their prayers are going unanswered, because God does not hear the prayers of sinners (Jn. 9:31). What they ask for, they are then asking for amiss and do not receive what they're asking for (James 4:3).

God's Word tells us that without faith it is IMPOSSIBLE to please God, we must not only believe that He is, but also that He is a Rewarder of those that diligently seek Him (Heb. 11:6). We must DILIGENTLY seek Him, not just occasionally, not just on Sunday, and not just when we are in need, or in trouble. We must seek Him at all times. To seek God is to seek a personal, intimate, loving relationship with Him, seek His instruction and guidance, not just His blessings. By diligently seeking Him, we hear His Word which contains all His laws, commandments, statutes and ordinances. To hear His Word means to hear it with our heart, not just our ears. By hearing His Word with our heart we gain faith (Rom. 10:17) through knowledge of the truth and the truth makes us free (Jn. 8:32). This in turn brings obedience to that faith (Rom. 1:1-5; 16:26).

Although it may not be one of the most popular messages, one message that needs to be preached truthfully in prison is, 'what does it mean to be "truly free."' *"If the Son therefore shall make you free, ye shall be free indeed." (Jn. 8:36)*. It is only by hearing the fullness of God's Word, the truth; that faith comes through understanding. God's Word tells us the truth shall make us free (Jn. 8:32), and that we shall be free indeed (Jn. 8:36). God's Word also tells us that Christ was sent to proclaim liberty to the captives, and the opening of the prison to them that are bound (Is. 61:1; Lk. 4:18). Often those who minister in prisons misrepresent and misuse these passages as though they are in reference to physical captivity and physical prisons, which they are not. Although God can, has, and does OCCASIONALLY deliver people from physical captivity and physical imprisonment, these passages are not in reference to that which is physical, but that which is spiritual. (Rom. 6:23) Spiritual captivity and being imprisoned in sin and the death sentence brought by breaking God's law, commandments, statutes and ordinances is far worse than any physical imprisonment. Anyone, sinner and saint alike, can be freed from physical imprisonment either through parole, commutation of sentence, or pardon. However, you cannot plea-bargain with God, there is no parole from the captivity and imprisonment of sin, and there is no commutation of sentence, there is only pardon by placing ones faith upon Jesus Christ and His sacrificial death. Because God loves each and every one of us, both those in prison and those outside of prison, He provided a way for us to be freed from the captivity of, imprisonment in, and the wages of our sin through Jesus Christ. Therefore, even if a person is never freed from their physical imprisonment, they are still 'free indeed;' right here and right now because our sin and the penalty of it has been pardoned by God through Christ even though we are still in physical imprisonment (Jn. 8:32, 36).

DELIVERANCE and INNER HEALING *(Luke 4:18, 19)*

Just as trouble comes in a lot of different ways, everyone's story/testimony is different. However, for those in prison, one thing is certain; at some point our story/testimony involved a head-on collision with the law. In order to receive deliverance and inner healing, it is necessary to revisit that particular time in our lives in self-reflection so that the issues which brought about the sin can be determined and scripturally dealt with. All too often we see people released from prison without ever being delivered and healed from the issues that brought about their incarceration.

Incarcerated people can, do, and will, face many complex issues such as; abandonment, from family, loved ones, and friends, prior to, during, and after prison. Sexual issues, forced sexual abuse, and self-inflicted sexual abuse in an environment wherein masturbation and homosexuality are often utilized as a coping mechanism. Depression and anxiety often leads to emotional issues, psychological issues, and suicide. Hopelessness, brought about by a lack of support. These are but a few of the many complex issues an incarcerated person has to face and most of the time they are forced to face these issues alone, without the aid of true spiritual guidance from those ministering to them.

Without properly researching what the Word of God reveals about these issues; individuals who face such issues are left to their own devise. It is for that very reason that most of these devastating issues are never truly scripturally dealt with and the person merely shuts down, puts on a mask, and keeps things bottled-up. Without the Word of God being ministered to them in truth, those ignorant of what God has to say about these issues are merely left ignorant, afraid to speak what is on their heart, afraid to express what they truly feel, and left hurting and wounded.

It is a proven fact that the vast majority of people in prison dwell in the past. They dwell on pain which stems from what went wrong in their life without being given a true step by step Biblical solution. And without this process, their deliverance, healing, and change will never come. This then fosters negative energy, a defeated attitude, and stagnate growth towards moving forward in Christ. Therefore, no "renewing of the mind" (Eph. 4:23; Rom. 12:2), and no restoration of joy (Ps. 51:12).

Although there are few that attempt to minister to those in great need of inner healing and deliverance, often their approach is a "One stop shopping, drive through service" approach which is inadequate and insufficient to truly meet the need. In ministering to a person in need of inner healing, and deliverance, there needs to be a more personal, in-depth approach taken in order for there to be any breakthrough. However, the general outlook of the Department of Corrections is one of restrictive limitation, and of boundaries and policies that by their very nature are designed to hinder that which is truly needed.

PREPARING TO LIVE SAVED IN A FREE SOCIETY, WHILE STILL INCARCERATED. *(2 Timothy 2:15)*.

Through experience, I have learned that those in prison are often arbitrarily categorized as hopeless, untrustworthy, and looked upon as a collective rather than as individuals. Those of us in prison are commonly all put into the same boat and looked upon through a tainted window, with a stereotypical tint, that gives a polluted perception of each person's potential as an individual. For this reason, jailhouse salvation, jailhouse lawyers, and anyone, or anything, coming from jail, or prison, is looked upon a lot more critically.

The very salvation of those saved while incarcerated is commonly looked upon skeptically, and a lot more critically, than others. Some skeptics have even outwardly stated, "It is easy to live the Christian life in a controlled environment because you don't have all the worlds' temptations." Many, having heard such statement, have felt that their very love for, faith in, and dedication to Jesus Christ and the Christian walk was being impugned (to attack by argument or criticism as false or questionable), simply because they are incarcerated. I too have previously taken these statements as a personal attack. However, when I examined the issue realistically and the reality of such a statement set in, I saw that the statement actually holds a lot of truth.

It was then, as an incarcerated man, that I began to think about just how to actually prepare to live the Christian life in the free society. You see those who are incarcerated have a tendency of doing things differently than those in the free society. Therefore, those things need to be changed right here, right now. It is while incarcerated that we need to take an honest look at ourselves and learn how to live the Christian life in a free society where the temptations are vastly more numerous than we now experience.

There have been countless numbers of unprepared Christians, who upon their release, have jumped right back into society and spiritually drowned. Totally unprepared to face what lies ahead, they tend to jump right into the deep end of the pool and drown spiritually. It is for this very reason that those ministering to prisoners need to begin the ministry of "teaching in preparation for release." in order to FULLY prepare those incarcerated for release into society. Many have been incarcerated for a long time and they need to be equipped for what they will be facing so they don't spiritually drown. I therefore encourage you to not make the same error as so many have and be either condescending, critical, or impugn (to attack by argument or criticism as false or questionable) the position in Christ of those incarcerated. Likewise true discernment must be utilized because there are also many that are incarcerated who are Spirit filled, gifted, talented, trained, and equipped ministers, preachers, and teachers who are currently active in the ministry both inside and outside of where they are incarcerated.

After spending a considerable amount of time in prison, I have found that there are those whose manner of thinking is not truly in touch with reality. Living in such a controlled environment can, and often does, give a false sense of reality. Men and women who will be reentering society after incarceration must therefore then be ministered to for the purpose of preparing them spiritually, mentally, and emotionally, in order to be able to handle a fast paced world and all the influences that come with it.

⇨ **The Way, the Truth, and the Life** *(John 14:5-14).*

Jesus is Truth-in-Action, so are we to be. In the sixth verse of John chapter fourteen, the pronouncement, "I Am," is threefold. It is only through Jesus that "the way" to God the

Father is made available. It is only Jesus who is the "truth" of God, revealing God the Father to us "in truth." It is also Jesus, who is the "life" of God that provided for us "life eternal." In 1 Peter 2:21-25, the Apostle Peter writes:

> *"For even hereunto were ye called: because Christ also suffered for us, leaving us an example, that ye should follow his steps:*
> *Who did no sin, neither was guile found in his mouth:*
> *Who, when he was reviled, reviled not again; when he suffered, he threatened not; but committed himself to him that judgeth righteously:*
> *Who his own self bar our sins in his own body on the tree; that we, being dead to sins, should live unto righteousness: by whose stripes ye were healed.*
> *For ye were sheep going astray; but are now returned unto the Shepherd and Bishop of your souls"* (I Peter 2:21 – 25)

⇨ **Facing Temptation** *(Matthew 4:1-11).*

Jesus was led by the Spirit into the desert to be tempted of the devil. After fasting for forty days Jesus was hungry. The devil looked upon this as an opportunity to tempt Jesus by first attempting to get Jesus to become selfishly prideful and "prove" He was the Son of God and command stones to be turned into bread, *"...If thou be the Son of God, command these stones be made bread"* (Mt. 4:3).

However, Jesus, confident in His relationship with God the Father, did not selfishly and nor prideful rise to the devil's challenge as the devil had hoped. Instead, Jesus turned the other cheek (Mt: 5:39), did not fight with the devil; but rather Jesus relied on the Word of God to OVERCOME the devil. *"But he answered and said, it is written, Man shall not live by bread alone, but by every word that proceeds out of the mouth of God."*

(John 4:4). At the time most people would have thought, like the devil did, that Jesus would have been the most vulnerable; however Jesus overcame the devil by not relying on what He heard, saw, or felt, but by relying on the Word of God. Here again, Jesus left us an example that we should follow in His steps (1 Peter 2:21-25). Just as Jesus Himself was tempted, all mankind will be tempted as well.

If we think that temptation will not come, we do nothing but deceive ourselves which makes it easier for us to succumb to temptation when it inevitably appears. This is especially true for Returning Citizens. After Jesus fasted forty days, hungry and deprived of food, the devil attacked with temptation after temptation. Likewise Returning Citizens who often been deprived of many things, hunger for the things of a free society that are now readily available to them. There are many temptations that follow release from incarceration, some small and some great. However, without being ministered to properly and taught how to battle these numerous temptations, they are ill prepared for such a battle and often fall in defeat.

⇨ **Repentance** *(Luke 13:3)*.

Repentance is far more than "feeling" sorry for something we have done, or failed to do. Repentance is truly "being" sorry for something we have done, or failed to do, and turning away from our wrongdoing, and turning toward God in obedience. The prophets urged God's people to turn from evil that they might know God.

> *"Therefore I will judge you, O house of Israel, every one according to his ways, saith the Lord God. Repent, and turn yourselves from all your transgressions; so iniquity shall not be your ruin. Cast away from you all your transgressions, whereby ye have transgressed; and make you a new heart and a new spirit: for why will ye die, O house of Israel? For I have*

no pleasure in the death of him that dieth, said the Lord God: wherefore turn yourselves, and live ye." (Ezekiel 18:30-32)

Likewise, Jesus Himself told us: "I come not to call the righteous, but sinners to repentance." (Luke 5:32)

⇨ **Forgiveness** *(Luke 17:3, 4)*

Jesus taught that to be forgiving is our duty and that there is to be no limit to the extent of our forgiveness.

"Take heed to yourselves: If thy brother trespass against thee, rebuke him; and if he repent, forgive him. And if he trespass against thee seven times in a day, and seven times in a day turn again to thee, saying, I repent; thou shalt forgive him." (Luke 17:3, 4).

Unforgiveness is of course a sin. Jesus warned us of the consequences of being unforgiving.

"For if ye forgive men their trepasses, your heavenly Father will also forgive you: But if ye forgive not men their trespasses, neither will your Father forgive your trespasses" (Matthew 6:14, 15)

Jesus also illustrated in Matthew 18:21-35 that the consequences of being unforgiving are severe. In Jesus' illustration a man who himself had been forgiven refused to likewise be forgiving and suffered greatly for his sin of unforgiveness. We as transgressors must repent and seek God's forgiveness and also the forgiveness of those we have wronged. It is our responsibility to seek the forgiveness of victims, family, loved ones, friends, and all those we have wronged through our former selfish, self-centered, disrespectful sinful behavior.

⇨ **Reconciliation *(2 Corinthians 5:17-20)*.**

Reconciliation is an important component of an obedient, faith filled, Christian walk. Reconciliation with God is imperative. The Apostle Paul writing to the Church at Corinth writes:

> *"Therefore if any man be in Christ, he is a new creature: old things are passed away; behold all things are become new. And all things are of God, who hath reconciled us to himself by Jesus Christ, and hath given to us the ministry of reconciliation; To wit, that God was in Christ, reconciling the world unto himself; not imputing their trespasses unto them; and hath committed unto us the word of reconciliation. Now then we are ambassadors for Christ, as though God did beseech you by us; we pray you in Christ's stead, be ye reconciled unto God." (2 Corinthians 5:17-20).*

Reconciliation is also imperative with family, loved ones, and friends (see 1 Corinthians 7:11; Matthew 5:24).

⇨ **Running a spiritual race after release (1 Corinthians 9:24-27).**

> *"Know ye not that they which run in a race run all, but one receiveth the prize? So run, that ye may obtain. And every man that striveth for the mastery is temperate in all things. Now they do it to obtain a corruptible crown; but we an incorruptible. I therefore so run, not as uncertainly; so fight I, not as one that beateth the air: But I keep under my body, and bring it into subjection: lest that by any means, when I have preached to others, I myself should be a castaway." (1 Corinthians 9:24-27).*

Running the Christian race in free society is vastly more challenging and difficult than it is while incarcerated. Although many have conditioned themselves to run the race, they have simply not been properly prepared with the crucial wisdom and support system they will need to run this race against the overwhelming odds they face. Everything is new to them and they haven't any idea of what truly lie before them, nor a realistic plan for survival. Those ministering to Returning Citizens should be preparing them for both the spiritual and practical sides of life on the outside. Those ministered to are repeatedly ministered to regarding the necessity and importance of a personal, intimate, loving relationship with God. They are ministered to regarding the impressiveness of living a wholesome Christian life and the race to be run. However, they are seldom, if ever, ministered to regarding just how to do so as they should. They are then only being given the wisdom of what has to be done, without being given the wisdom of how to accomplish it. It is like starting a race without knowing that there is a set course that has to be run and how to run that course.

The running of this spiritual race to the finish line is imperative and there is no reward for those that fall short. The race that we run is likewise not a sprint; it is a lifelong marathon. For those released from incarceration - there are two legs to this marathon. The first leg is run while incarcerated, the second begins the minute they are released. Time after time we hear of Christian men and women who step up to the starting line of the second leg of race (the prison door). The prison official announces, "On your mark, ready, set, GO, GO, GO!" The Christians heart pounds and their breathing quickens as they race past the starting line, every fiber in their being straining and rushing forward. While incarcerated they spent years conditioning themselves for this very moment and now they are in the most important race of their lives. Now they run, for all they are worth they run, but wait, something's wrong, no one explained to them the course they are to run. No one told them that their first and most important rest stop was a right turn into a church, the house of God. No one told them they would need the strength and support they could only get by running straight to the house of God and kneeling before the altar to give thanks and receive the support they need. Therefore, instead of making that important right turn, they make a wrong turn and run in the wrong direction. Instead of their first rest stop being the house of God, they stop at momma's house, or their spouses' house, a friends' house, restaurant or any number of places (Lk. 14:33; Mt. 10:37 - 38; 19:29). The next thing you know, the strength they began this leg of the race with is gone. Their race slows and they fall flat on their face. They try to crawl to the finish line but it's just not possible, it's simply too far away. If they had only been ministered to correctly. If they had only been properly prepared, their race would not have ended in vain.

BREAKING THE CYCLE OF INCARCERATION

In order to break the cycle of incarceration one must be totally sold-out for Jesus and become Righteous, Upright, Honorable, and Free from wrongdoing. Righteousness contains the virtuous attributes of: love, joy, peace, longsuffering, gentleness, goodness, faith, meekness, and temperance (Gal. 5:22-25). Just as God Himself is righteous, He demands us to likewise be righteous (Mt. 9:13; 13:43; 25:46; Rom. 5:19; James. 5:16; 1 Jn. 2:28, 29; 3:7).

The revolving door of prison is constantly turning. It is a vicious cycle that must be stopped. This can only be accomplished through purposeful ministering and proper planning for living a godly, goal oriented, crime free life, wherein failure is not an option.

Dedication and commitment to being successful must begin while still incarcerated. An important key to a successful transition is to establish and reestablish relationships with family, church members, and community leaders. Absent a true faith based support system, there is a much greater chance of slipping in our walk with God when released. Without the support they need, Returning Citizens are a lot more likely to slip back into former things, back into the grasp of hell and back into prison.

Another very important part of breaking the cycle is to remain mindful of the past. Often when released, Returning Citizens return to either the same inappropriate places and associates, or the same type of inappropriate places and associates that formerly were contributing factors in their sin and incarceration.

⇨ **New Wine In Old Wineskins (Mark 2:22).**

"And no one pours new wine into old wineskins. If he does, the wine will burst the skins, and both the wine and the wineskins will be ruined. No, he pours new wine into new wineskins." (Mark 2:22)

Jesus came to offer a new life imparted by faith in Him, and the joy of the new message cannot be lived in the old ways of the past. God's Word tells us that we are a new creature (2 Cor. 5:17) and as such we are to walk in the newness of life (Rom. 6:4). Therefore, as a new creature in Christ (the new wine), we are not to be put into old wineskins (the old ways of life), we are to live in the newness of life (new wineskins) and not return to the former ways which resulted in failure (the wineskin bursting).

⇨ **Wise and Foolish Builders (Luke 6:46-49).**

"And why call ye me, Lord, Lord, and do not the things which I say? Whosoever cometh to me, and heareth my sayings, and doeth them, I will show you to whom he is like: He is like a man which built a house, and digged deep, and laid the foundation on a rock; and when the flood arose, the stream beat vehemently upon that house, and could not shake it: for it was founded upon a rock. But he that heareth, and doeth not, is like a man

that without a foundation built a house upon the earth; against which the stream did beat vehemently, and immediately it fell; and the ruin of that house great." (Luke 6:46 – 49)

As Jesus illustrates in the parable of the Wise and Foolish builders, we see that it is God's will for us to build our house on the foundation of the Rock (revelation knowledge given by God (Mt. 16:17, 18)), and not on the earth (our former foundation).

MENTORING INCARCERATED SAINTS.

There are many ways in which incarcerated saints can be mentored, seminary classes and training, clergy visits, letters, etc., just to name a few. Mentoring can be a very beneficial means to nurture and help develop incarcerated saints. To do so, requires a power-free relationship based upon trust and respect between two people. In this relationship there must be mutual respect between the mentor, (who is generally more spiritually mature and experienced), and the mentee who is being developed in character and competence.

Why mentor? Mentoring provides a positive influence on those incarcerated by outside ministers, who have a great influence on those inside. This powerful, motivating influence can help Returning Citizens create and meet goals in life, based upon godliness and wisdom. Those who are mentored are thereby less likely to relapse into their former sinful and criminal ways. Likewise, by being mentored, they are more likely to stay faithful to the Word of God, raise their families in godliness, hold a job, and contribute to society themselves by mentoring and being involved in community programs that enhance social well-being.

Although mentoring an incarcerated person may at first seem intimidating, you will soon see just how rewarding it can be. Giving someone the support and guidance they need to make right choices and seeing the benefit of your efforts rewarded as they move toward and achieve their goals can be very thrilling and spiritually rewarding.

We see in the Apostle Paul a great example of mentorship. When Paul went to Derbe and Lystra he came upon a disciple named Timothy, whose mother was a believing Jewess, but his father was Greek. Paul stepped into the role of mentor and took Timothy with him (Acts 16:1, 3). As Timothy's mentor, Paul became a spiritual father and Timothy became his son (1 Tim. 1:2; Phil. 2:22). Paul's efforts were greatly rewarded when he saw in Timothy the same unfeigned faith that Timothy's grandmother Lois, and mother Eunice possessed (2 Tim. 1:5). Paul then encouraged Timothy to stir up the gift of God within him, received by the laying on of Paul's hands (Paul's active participation as a mentor) (2 Tim. 1:6). Paul also mentored Titus in the same way (Titus 1:4). Because Paul took an active hands-on role in the lives of Timothy and Titus as their mentor, they became powerful men of God and went on to do great things.

A mentoring ministry should be one that helps those that are incarcerated become connected to the body of Christ (the Church) outside of the prison walls by giving them a church home in the community. Churches that are going to begin mentorship ministries should have those that are willing to be mentors undergo training so that they will be effective in doing ministry decently and in order. An effective mentor is one who:

- ✓ Is a good, active listener.
- ✓ Has and demonstrate genuine interest.
- ✓ Encourages and demonstrates confidence in those being mentored.
- ✓ Exhibits patience, and kindness.
- ✓ Recognizes mentee as an individual.
- ✓ Is loyal, honest, and trustworthy of what should be held in confidence.
- ✓ Is interested in sharing knowledge and experiences, including successes and failures.

- ✓ Has a good sense of humor and is personable.
- ✓ Is willing to motivate and help mentee to learn and grow.
- ✓ Is helpful, assisting those incarcerated reconnect with their children and family through spiritual and social guidance.

It should also be taken into consideration, mentoring the children of those incarcerated. Children who have an incarcerated parent/parents have a 70% chance of ending up in prison themselves.

COUNTY JAIL MINISTRY -vs- PRISON MINISTRY

Jail and Prison, although similar, differ in a few points.

COUNTY JAIL. Let me begin by saying that there are some people who have truly been converted while in the county jail. However, for the most part, from the moment that most people are arrested for committing crime(s) they are sorry, sorry they got caught, not necessarily sorry for what they did. Many of them attempt to cut a deal or plea-bargain with God, immediately cry out, *"God, please help me. Lord Jesus, if You will get me out of this I will...."* It is for this reason that many begin attending church services in jail. Most individuals, who attend church services in jail, pray and read their Bibles. However, most often they do so merely in an attempt to get a "Get out of jail free card." While in jail, as they are going through the trial for their crime(s), they faithfully attend church services, read their Bible, and pray, pray, pray! That is, until they find that God did not accept the deal they tried to cut, nor their plea bargain. At that point a large percentage of them throw the Bible down in anger and turn their back on God. Many have stated, "I tried that Jesus stuff and it didn't work. I went to church, read the Bible, and prayed every day. Yet, here I am in prison anyway, that religious stuff doesn't work!" Many people have tried that 'religious stuff' both those incarcerated and those who are not. Often people view

God as a holy puppet on a string that you can make move through 'religious stuff.' However, God will not be mocked. God is love and His desire is to give His love and all that comes with it, to those that will love Him in return and give themselves to Him, not those that do religious acts. Religious acts are no substitute for a personal, intimate, loving relationship. However, it is important that I also remind you that there are some who, while in the county jail, were truly converted and who serve God with a sincere heart and who have remained faithful to God no matter what the outcome of their trial.

PRISON. For those in prison who attend church services, their reality is different. They have already had a trial, received their punishment/sentence, and have had time to evaluate their former life. They have accepted responsibility for their actions and do not blame anyone, any situation, or society for the wrong decisions they made that placed them in prison. They are truly sorrowful and sincerely repentant for their sinful disobedience to God, the harm they have done and the burden they have placed on their victim(s), their families, and society. Now in their repentance, they strive to be a blessing instead of a hindrance in peoples' lives and to never hurt anyone in any way, shape, or fashion ever again.

Although there may be a few exceptions, the vast majority of those you minister to in prison have a positive and optimistic attitude. In their sincere effort to learn God's ways, obedience, and faith, it is their full intent to go from glory to glory. Therefore, their days are filled with preparation, studying the Word of God, and making gifts, skills, and talents in order to be used of God in their calling upon release.

It is also safe to say that those in prison who have been incarcerated for many years, daydream and wonder about what life will be like when released. Life of course, will be vastly different from anything they have previously known. They will now be serving God and living in a world that is far different than what they have known. Not only have they changed, but the world and society has also changed over the years. For some, this is where the dream of being released and working in the ministry and etc. can become a fantasy. Those in prison tend to have everything mapped-out in their heads: they believe they are on track to be the best husband/wife, or parent, their children are going to be good, everything is going to be just perfect in this wonderful world they have created in their minds. However, the reality of the real world is that life comes at you fast and with it comes many pros and cons.

A calling to minister to those in jail or prison, as I previously have said, is a special and unique calling in the ministry, however, knowing who you are ministering to, what their true needs are, and how to meet those needs, is half the battle.

DATING & COURTING IN THE CHURCH

<u>Dating</u> is an appointment, especially an engagement to go out socially with another person. <u>Courting</u> is (1) to try to win the favor of by attention or flattery, (2) to try to win the affections or love of, (3) to attempt to gain: seek, and (4) to behave so as to invite or incur. <u>To woo</u> is to flatter solicitously in an attempt to obtain something or remove antagonism.

We have heard the definitions, now let's get real on the subject of romantically dating and courting. There have been reports of those getting out of prison and crossing the line (fornication within the church). Most of those who have gotten saved on the inside, come out of prison knowing what it is like to date and court before being saved, but after years of not being able to interact romantically with the opposite sex, there can be a real temptation and challenge. The challenge is two-fold when returning home from prison there is a transitional period that has to take place for most, which is: (1) getting used to being free again, and (2) learning to walk according to God's Word and Will for the first time in the free world.

Dating and courting in church is not just an issue and concern for those getting out of prison, but also for other single brothers and sisters seeking to find a mate. Each church may have their own criteria on dating and courting. Some feel dating leads to mating and that could likely be courting disaster within the church.

The Bible does not mention dating per se in Biblical times, but there are several mentions of courtship. Courtship was the period of engagement which was part of the ritual of marriage. With most marriages in Biblical times being arranged marriages, dating, courting was the way of finding a mate (husband/wife); today is a little different, which may be the reason why over 50% of marriages end up in divorce in the church and even higher for those not in the church. Learning how to find a mate in the church is a big issue for everyone, but even more so for those coming out of prison that have been deprived of sex. Now that they are saved and free, they want to have sex. And this burning desire may urge some to cross the line or rush into a marriage just to have sex. For the most part, Saints coming out of prison want to live clean before the Lord and not have sex out of wedlock, but it needs to be ministered on.

MEN AND WOMEN IN PRISON MINISTRY

Laborers in the vineyard have a mission to do the work of the ministry they are called to do. Just as Jesus sent out the twelve disciples, He instructed them concerning the foundation of their mission, the substance of their message, the works they were to perform, the equipment they were to take, and their procedure. As a representative of the Church and not just your local church, but the body of Christ, the mission of the disciples foreshadowed the ongoing mission of the church.

It is God's desire that all men be saved and that none should perish, and that they should all come into the knowledge of the truth (1 Timothy 2:3, 4). Yet, as we are told in Romans 10:14, 15 this cannot take place without a preacher being sent. However, at some point there has to be a time wherein the foundation that has been built, is built upon truth, and those who are now able to eat meat, receive meat and not continuously milk. It is true that not everyone is going to be saved and come into the knowledge of the truth. However, let us not grow weary while doing good for in due season we shall reap if we do not lose heart (Galatians 6:9).

My brothers and sisters in the ministry, I bid you God speed as you follow the leading and guidance of the Holy Spirit. Be strong in the Lord and the power of His might!

If you have any questions or comments, please feel free to contact me at:

Raymond L. Carr, Jr. #232256
(Due to consistent movement of the MDOC inmates; please search my current location under www.michigan.gov/OTIS)

Made in the USA
Charleston, SC
06 January 2016